CW00662971

Every Cloud has a Silver Lining

EVERY CLOUD HAS A SILVER LINING

This edition copyright © Summersdale Publishers Ltd, 2016
First published in 2012

Summersdale Publishers Ltd
46 West Street
Chichester
West Sussex
PO19 1RP
UK

www.summersdale.com

Printed and bound in the Czech Republic

ISBN: 978-1-84953-908-1

Substantial discounts on bulk quantities of Summersdale books are available to corporations, professional associations and other organisations. For details contact general enquiries: telephone: +44 (0) 1243 771107 or email: enquiries@summersdale.com.

Every Cloud has a Silver Lining

summersdale

Storms make oaks
take deeper root.

George Herbert

IF YOU'RE ALREADY WALKING ON THIN ICE, YOU MIGHT AS WELL DANCE.

Proverb

Start each
day with
a positive
thought

Even if you fall on
your face, you're still
moving forward.

Robert C. Gallagher

I'M NOT AFRAID
of storms, for I'm
learning how
TO SAIL
my ship.

Louisa May Alcott

Happiness is not
an ideal of reason,
but of imagination.

Immanuel Kant

FAILURE IS ANOTHER STEPPING STONE TO GREATNESS.

Oprah Winfrey

The optimist sees the doughnut; the pessimist sees the hole.

Anonymous

Rain is just confetti from the sky

Perhaps our eyes need to be washed by our tears once in a while, so that we can see life with a clearer view again.

Alex Tan

Whether you think
you can or think you
can't – you're right.

Henry Ford

Positive mind,
positive vibes,
positive life

Keep a
GREEN TREE
in your heart
and perhaps
a singing bird
WILL COME.

Chinese proverb

If we had no winter, the
spring would not be
so pleasant; if we did
not sometimes taste of
adversity, prosperity
would not be so welcome.

Anne Bradstreet

Say yes
to new
adventures

I am an optimist. It does not seem too much use being anything else.

Winston Churchill

When asked if my cup is
half-full or half-empty my
only response is that I am
thankful I have a cup.

Anonymous

ANGELS
CAN FLY
BECAUSE
THEY TAKE
THEMSELVES
LIGHTLY.

G. K. Chesterton

There is always a bright side

The misfortunes hardest to bear are those which never come.

Amy Lowell

Whenever you fall,
pick something up.

Oswald Avery

Stay sunny
on the inside

A positive attitude will not solve all your problems, but it will annoy other people enough to make it worth the effort.

Herm Albright

Life isn't about WAITING FOR THE storm to pass; it's about learning to dance IN THE RAIN.

Vivian Greene

If it doesn't
challenge
you, it
doesn't
change you

The best way to cheer
yourself up is to cheer
someone else up.

Mark Twain

THE DARKEST
HOUR HAS ONLY
60 MINUTES.

Morris Mandel

Since the house is on fire
let us warm ourselves.

Italian proverb

In the land of the blind,
the one-eyed man is king.

Erasmus

WHEREVER YOU GO,
no matter what
the weather,
ALWAYS BRING YOUR
own sunshine.

Anthony J. D'Angelo

Positive anything is better than negative nothing.

Elbert Hubbard

Dare to begin

AN ADVENTURE IS ONLY
AN INCONVENIENCE
RIGHTLY CONSIDERED.
AN INCONVENIENCE IS
ONLY AN ADVENTURE
WRONGLY CONSIDERED.

G. K. Chesterton

You may not realise it
when it happens, but
a kick in the teeth may
be the best thing in
the world for you.

Walt Disney

ATTITUDE IS A LITTLE THING THAT MAKES A BIG DIFFERENCE.

Winston Churchill

I don't think of all the misery, but of the beauty that still remains.

Anne Frank

It always seems impossible until it is done

Nothing is a waste of
time if you use the
experience wisely.

Auguste Rodin

LIFE IS EITHER A DARING ADVENTURE OR NOTHING.

Helen Keller

The best way to secure future happiness is to be as happy as is rightfully possible today.

Charles W. Eliot

Splash around
in life's
puddles

Happiness consists not in having much, but being content with little.

Marguerite Gardiner

TO CLIMB
steep hills
requires slow
pace at first.

William Shakespeare

You can't be brave if you've only had wonderful things happen to you.

Mary Tyler Moore

Be happy. It's one
way of being wise.

Colette

It's always darkest just before the dawn

But the man worth while is the one who will smile, when everything goes dead wrong.

Ella Wheeler Wilcox

There are always
flowers for those who
want to see them.

Henri Matisse

A happy life consists not in the absence, but in the mastery of hardships.

Helen Keller

AERODYNAMICALLY
THE BUMBLEBEE
SHOULDN'T BE ABLE
TO FLY, BUT THE
BUMBLEBEE DOESN'T
KNOW SO IT GOES ON
FLYING ANYWAY.

Mary Kay Ash

All great achievements
require time.

Maya Angelou

IT'S OK TO HAVE
BUTTERFLIES IN
YOUR STOMACH.
JUST GET THEM TO
FLY IN FORMATION.

Rob Gilbert

Dreams are renewable.
No matter what our
age or condition, there
are still untapped
possibilities within us.

Dave Turner

Don't be the same – be better

A man's reach should
exceed his grasp,
Or what's a heaven for?

Robert Browning

The grand essentials to happiness in this life are: something to do, something to love and something to hope for.

George Washington Burnap

keep hope in your heart

In the middle of difficulty
lies opportunity.

Albert Einstein

To me,
every hour
of the day
AND NIGHT
is an unspeakably
perfect miracle.

Walt Whitman

One may walk over
the highest mountain
one step at a time.

John Wanamaker

Without the rain there would never be rainbows

Become a possibilitarian.
No matter how dark
things seem or actually
are, raise your sights and
see the possibilities.

Norman Vincent Peale

Bad days
help you
appreciate
the good
ones

A strong positive attitude
will create more miracles
than any wonder drug.

Patricia Neal

In three words I can sum up everything I've learned about life: it goes on.

Robert Frost

IT JUST WOULDN'T BE A PICNIC WITHOUT THE ANTS.

Anonymous

Having a positive mental
attitude is asking how
something can be done
rather than saying
it can't be done.

Bo Bennett

Inhale
confidence,
exhale doubt

Find ecstasy in life;
the mere sense of
living is joy enough.

Emily Dickinson

Mighty oaks FROM little acorns grow.

Anonymous

Turn your face to the
sun and the shadows
fall behind you.

Maori proverb

The more we are aware
of to be grateful for, the
happier we become.

Ezra Taft Benson

Be positive,
patient and
persistent

Those who bring sunshine into the lives of others cannot keep it from themselves.

J. M. Barrie

A CERTAIN AMOUNT
OF OPPOSITION
IS A GREAT HELP
TO A MAN. KITES
RISE AGAINST, NOT
WITH THE WIND.

John Neal

Your attitude can take you
forward or your attitude
can take you down. The
choice is always yours!

Catherine Pulsifer

I have found that if
you love life, life will
love you back.

Arthur Rubenstein

Always laugh
when you can.
IT IS CHEAP
MEDICINE.

Lord Byron

Find joy in
the ordinary

The robbed that smiles,
steals something
from the thief.

William Shakespeare

If you're going through hell, keep going.

Winston Churchill

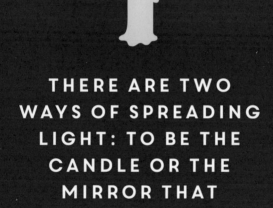

THERE ARE TWO
WAYS OF SPREADING
LIGHT: TO BE THE
CANDLE OR THE
MIRROR THAT
REFLECTS IT.

Edith Wharton

It's all about the way you look at it

Some days you're the bug. Some days you're the windshield.

Price Cobb

There is no failure except
in no longer trying.

Elbert Hubbard

Accept what
is, let go of
what was,
have faith in
what will be

Success is due less to
ability than to zeal.

Charles Buxton

The power
of imagination
MAKES US INFINITE.

John Muir

Dwell in
possibility

The tests of life are not
meant to break you,
but to make you.

Norman Vincent Peale

Have patience and endure:
this unhappiness will
one day be beneficial.

Ovid

See the light
in others

No life is so hard that
you can't make it easier
by the way you take it.

Ellen Glasgow

WE ARE ALL IN THE
GUTTER BUT SOME
OF US ARE LOOKING
AT THE STARS.

Oscar Wilde

Be kind to
yourself

All the statistics in the
world can't measure the
warmth of a smile.

Chris Hart

PROBLEMS ARE
opportunities
WITH
thorns
ON THEM.

Hugh Miller

Happiness is like a butterfly which, when pursued, is always beyond our grasp, but, if you will sit down quietly, may alight upon you.

Nathaniel Hawthorne

SOME DAYS THERE WON'T BE A SONG IN YOUR HEART. SING ANYWAY.

Emory Austin

Toughness is in
the soul and spirit,
not in muscles.

Alex Karras

Hold on to
the good
things

No problem can withstand the assault of sustained thinking.

Voltaire

The very best proof
that something can be
done is that someone
has already done it.

Bertrand Russell

No one knows
WHAT HE CAN DO
until
he tries.

Publilius Syrus

All that I can, I will.

Frε̄nch proverb

Don't forget
to stop and
smell the
roses

YOU'RE THE BLACKSMITH OF YOUR OWN HAPPINESS.

Swedish proverb

You can have anything
you want if you give
up the belief that
you can't have it.

Robert Anthony

The way I see it,
IF YOU WANT
the rainbow,
you gotta put up
WITH THE RAIN.

Dolly Parton

Fall seven times,
stand up eight.

Japanese proverb

You don't have to be perfect to be amazing

Defeat is not bitter
unless you swallow it.

Joe Clark

Against the assault of laughter, nothing can stand.

Mark Twain

Believe with all of your
heart that you will do what
you were made to do.

Orison Swett Marden

Choose
kindness and
laugh often

What seems to us as bitter trials are often blessings in disguise.

Oscar Wilde

THE BEST
WAY OUT IS
ALWAYS
THROUGH.

Robert Frost

Don't get your knickers
in a knot. Nothing is
solved and it just makes
you walk funny.

Kathryn Carpenter

IF THE SKIES FALL, ONE MAY HOPE TO CATCH LARKS.

François Rabelais

you always
have a choice

Life shrinks or expands
in proportion to
one's courage.

Anais Nin

I CAN'T CHANGE
the direction
of the wind
but I can
ADJUST MY SAILS
to reach my
destination.

Jimmy Dean

If you don't like something, change it; if you can't change it, change the way you think about it.

Mary Engelbreit

OPPORTUNITY'S
FAVOURITE DISGUISE
IS TROUBLE.

Frank Tyger

Choose to be happy

We are all alike
on the inside.

Mark Twain

Good things take time

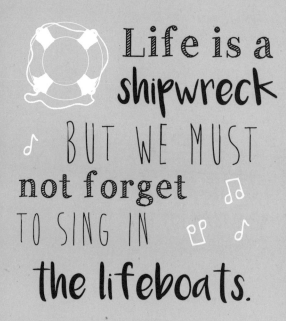

Life is a shipwreck BUT WE MUST not forget TO SING IN the lifeboats.

Voltaire

Look at everything as
though you were seeing
it for the first or last time.

Betty Smith

BEING IN A
GOOD FRAME
OF MIND HELPS
ONE KEEP IN
THE PICTURE
OF HEALTH.

Anonymous

If you call a thing bad you do little, if you call a thing good you do much.

Johann Wolfgang von Goethe

If the wind will not serve, TAKE TO THE OARS.

Latin proverb

How far that little candle
throws his beams!
So shines a good deed
in a naughty world.

William Shakespeare

THERE ARE EXACTLY AS MANY SPECIAL OCCASIONS IN LIFE AS WE CHOOSE TO CELEBRATE.

Robert Brault

Nobody can go back and start a new beginning, but anyone can start today and make a new ending.

Maria Robinson

There are
secret
opportunities
hidden inside
every setback

If we take the good
we find, asking no
questions, we shall have
heaping measures.

Ralph Waldo Emerson

your attitude
is everything

Every thought is a seed. IF YOU PLANT crab apples, DON'T COUNT ON harvesting Golden Delicious.

Bill Meyer

Be glad of life because it
gives you the chance to
love, to work, to play and
to look up at the stars.

Henry van Dyke

Even bees,
the little almsmen
OF SPRING BOWERS,
know there is
richest juice
IN POISON-FLOWERS.

John Keats

Anywhere you go liking
everyone, everyone
will be likable.

Mignon McLaughlin

Say good
words, think
good things,
do good
deeds

Do something wonderful.
People may imitate it.

Albert Schweitzer

We can always learn something from life's lessons

Heaven is under our feet
as well as over our heads.

Henry David Thoreau

THINK BIG
THOUGHTS
but relish
small pleasures.

H. Jackson Brown Jr

Laughter is a sunbeam
of the soul.

Thomas Mann

Do all things
with love

LET THE RAIN
BEAT UPON YOUR
HEAD WITH SILVER
LIQUID DROPS,
LET THE RAIN SING
YOU A LULLABY.

Langston Hughes

Don't fear change.
It's always for the best.

Richard Bach

Do something today that your future self will thank you for

Happiness often sneaks in through a door you didn't know you left open.

John Barrymore

Every cloud
has a silver
lining

Image credits

p.3 and throughout – sun behind cloud –
© Summersdale Publishers Ltd

p.5 – © Ekaterina Garyuk/Shutterstock.com

p.8 – clouds – © Summersdale Publishers Ltd;
p.8 – wind – © Vector Tradition SM/Shutterstock.com;
p.8 – ship's wheel – © Wiktoria Matynia/Shutterstock.com

p.10 – © Summersdale Publishers Ltd

p.16 – tree – © Iriskana/Shutterstock.com;
p.16 – sun – © Art'nLera/Shutterstock.com;
p.16 – bird – © basel101658/Shutterstock.com

p.21 – © Alika-Dream/Shutterstock.com

p.27 – clouds – © Summersdale Publishers Ltd;
p.27 – raincoat – © Ksena Shu/Shutterstock.com;
p.27 – raindrops – © vectorEps/Shutterstock.com

p.30 – © Leremy/Shutterstock.com

p.33 – © Art'nLera/Shutterstock.com

p.36 – © Uncle Leo/Shutterstock.com

p.38 – birds – © Yurchenko Yulia/Shutterstock.com;
p.38 – musical notes – © lineartestpilot/Shutterstock.com

p.42 – © Happy Art/Shutterstock.com

p.46 – shoeprints – © halimqd/Shutterstock.com;
p.46 – mountain – © VoodooDot/Shutterstock.com;
p.46 – tortoise – © Benjavisa Ruangvaree/Shutterstock.com

p.53 – © Lorelyn Medina/Shutterstock.com

p.55 – © Summersdale Publishers Ltd

p.62 – clock – © TashaNatasha/Shutterstock.com;
p.62 – stars – © T-Kot/Shutterstock.com

p.69 – sandwich – © Ohn Mar/Shutterstock.com;
p.69 – ants – © BestVectorIcon/Shutterstock.com

p.73 – tree – © BEYOND GRAPHICS/Shutterstock.com

For more information about our books, find us on Facebook at **Summersdale Publishers** and follow us on Twitter at **@Summersdale**.

www.summersdale.com